Cupcake Cakes

Lisa Turner Anderson

Photographs by Zac Williams

GIBBS SMITH
TO ENRICH AND INSPIRE HUMANKIND

To my parents

First Edition
15 14 13 12 11   5 4 3 2 1

Text © 2011 Lisa Turner Anderson
Photographs © 2011 Zac Williams

Published by
Gibbs Smith
P.O. Box 667
Layton, Utah 84041

1.800.835.4993 orders
www.gibbs-smith.com

Designed by Dawn DeVries Sokol
Manufactured in Shenzhen, China, in December 2010 by Toppan Printing Co.

Gibbs Smith books are printed on either recycled, 100% post-consumer waste,
FSC-certified papers or on paper produced from sustainable PEFC-certified forest/
controlled wood source. Learn more at www.pefc.org.

Library of Congress Cataloging-in-Publication Data

Anderson, Lisa Turner.
  Cupcake cakes / Lisa Turner Anderson ; photographs by Zac Williams.
      p. cm.
  ISBN 978-1-4236-1748-8
  1. Cupcakes. 2. Cookbooks. I. Williams, Zac. II. Title.
  TX771.A575 2011
  641.8'653—dc22
                        2010035249

Contents

Introduction

Using cupcakes is an easy and fun way to create cakes in all shapes and sizes! Cupcakes are like building blocks that you can put together in lots of different ways, meaning you can make all kinds of shaped cakes without having to use special pans. Plus, cupcakes are easy to serve and fun to eat! Before you get started making these great cakes for your friends, your family, and yourself, read the following tips to make sure your cakes are a success.

Baking the Cupcakes

You can use any recipe or any flavor of cake mix to make the cupcakes. A cake mix will make 24 cupcakes or 48 mini cupcakes. If you're making cupcakes from scratch, check the recipe for the number of cupcakes or mini cupcakes it makes. Most of the cakes in this book use fewer than 24 regular size or 48 mini cupcakes, but some of the larger cakes use more. Make sure to check the recipe in this book to see if you will need more batter than one cake mix or recipe will make.

For mini cupcakes, you'll just need to buy a mini muffin tin, which you can get anywhere kitchen supplies are sold. Mini cupcakes will only need to bake about 10 minutes in the oven.

When baking cupcakes, always use paper liners. That way you don't have to grease the pans, and the cupcakes will come out easily.

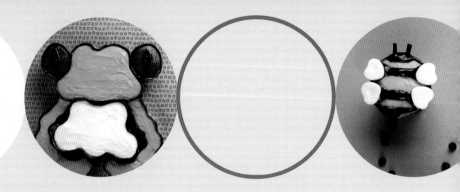

Frosting

To decorate the cupcakes in this book, you can use either canned store-bought frosting or homemade buttercream frosting, which is a bit stiffer than canned frosting. When using a decorating bag and tip, you'll need a stiffer frosting.

Vanilla Buttercream Frosting

- ½ cup butter, softened
- 1 teaspoon vanilla
- 4 cups powdered sugar
- 3 tablespoons milk

1 In a large bowl, beat together butter and vanilla with an electric mixer.

2 Add powdered sugar to butter mixture, one cup at a time, alternating with one tablespoon milk. Beat until smooth.

Chocolate Buttercream Frosting

- ½ cup butter, softened
- 1 teaspoon vanilla
- 4 cups powdered sugar
- ⅔ cup cocoa powder
- 5 tablespoons milk

1 In a large bowl, beat together butter and vanilla with an electric mixer.

2 Whisk together powdered sugar and cocoa. Add dry mixture to butter mixture, one cup at a time, alternating with one tablespoon milk. Beat until smooth.

Coloring Your Frosting

Decorating cakes is a lot more fun with colorful frosting! For pale or pastel colors, you can use liquid food coloring from the grocery store. But for deeper, brighter colors, you'll need to buy gel

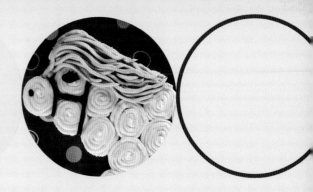

food coloring at a cake decorating or craft store. Gel food coloring comes in lots of colors and is very concentrated, so you don't have to use much to get a bright color.

Use a craft stick or toothpick to add gel food coloring to frosting. Add just a little bit at a time until you get the color you want.

Black Frosting

Many of the recipes in this book call for black frosting. If only a little bit is needed, the ingredients list will call for a tube of black gel frosting. You can buy black gel frosting at grocery stores. If the recipe needs a lot of black frosting, the best way to make it is to start with chocolate frosting and add black gel food coloring. If you do that you'll need to use a lot less black gel food coloring than if you were starting with vanilla frosting.

Decorating the Cakes

For most of the recipes in this book, you'll need to use frosting to draw lines or shapes on the cakes. You can use a decorating bag and a round tip, which you can purchase at some grocery stores or anywhere cake decorating supplies are sold. If you don't have a decorating bag, you can simply spoon the frosting into a ziplock bag and snip off a corner with scissors. For some of the recipes, though, you'll need a special decorating tip such as a star or flower. For those recipes, you will need a decorating bag.

Candy is a fun and colorful way to add designs and details to your cakes. If you have an idea for a different color or shape of candy than the book calls for, go for it! Use your imagination, be creative, and most of all, have fun!

Cute Caterpillar

- 11 cupcakes
- Green frosting
- Yellow Mike and Ike candies
- Yellow frosting
- Purple Wild Berry Skittles
- White frosting
- Purple Spree candies
- Yellow Dum-Dums

1 Frost the cupcakes with green frosting. Arrange the cupcakes in a caterpillar shape. Stick yellow Mike and Ike candies into the bottom of the cupcakes for the feet.

2 Place the yellow frosting in a decorating bag with a round tip or a ziplock bag with the corner snipped off. Draw a circle on each of the cupcakes, except for the head. Place a purple Skittle in the center of each yellow circle.

3 Place the white frosting in a decorating bag with a round tip or a ziplock bag with the corner snipped off. Draw eyes on the caterpillar's face. Place a purple Spree candy on each white circle and use more white frosting to make pupils. Draw a smile. Stick yellow Dum-Dums into the head for antennae.

Ice Cream Cone

- 18 mini cupcakes
- Chocolate frosting
- Pink frosting
- Red frosting
- Good & Fruity candy
- Chocolate chunks
- Sour straws

1 Frost 10 cupcakes with chocolate frosting. Frost 7 cupcakes with pink frosting. Frost the remaining cupcake with red frosting.

2 Arrange the chocolate-frosted cupcakes in an ice cream cone shape by making a row of 4 cupcakes, then a row of 3, then a row of 2, then 1. Make the scoop of ice cream by placing a row of 4 cupcakes with pink frosting above the top of the cone. Place a row of 3 cupcakes with pink frosting above that. Place the cupcake with the red frosting at the top.

3 Place chocolate frosting in a decorator's bag with a round tip or a ziplock bag with the corner snipped off. Outline the cone shapes with frosting, then pipe 3 diagonal lines across the cones in each direction.

4 Sprinkle Good & Fruity candies on the pink ice cream cone. Place a piece of green sour straw in the red cupcake for the cherry stem.

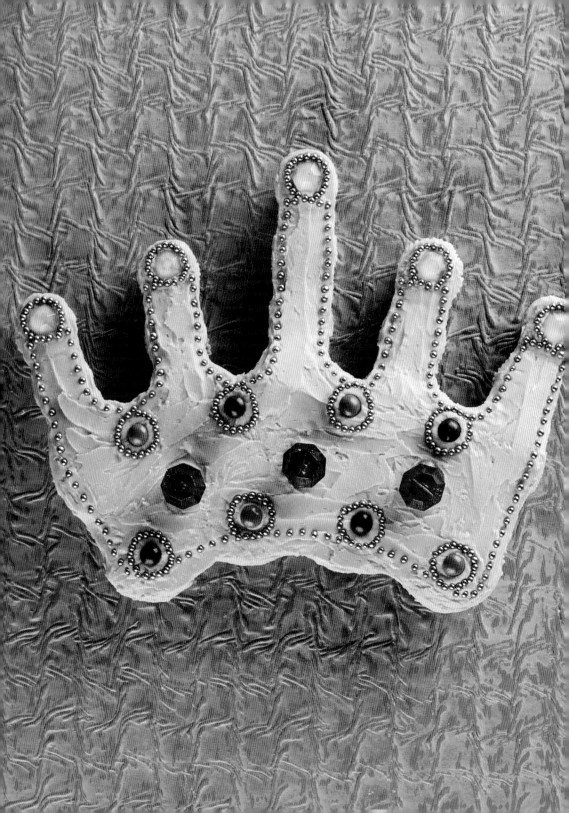

Pink Princess Crown

1 Frost all the cupcakes with pink frosting.
Arrange the cupcakes in a crown shape by placing 4 at the bottom in an arched shape, then 5 above that. Place 3 mini cupcakes vertically above the center cupcake. Place 2 mini cupcakes vertically above each of the remaining 4 cupcakes.

2 Stick the plastic part of the Ring Pops into the gaps between the bottom row of cupcakes and the row above. Cover the plastic with pink frosting. Cover any remaining gaps between cupcakes with pink frosting.

3 Outline the crown with silver dragées as shown in photo.

4 Add pink and purple skittles to the crown as shown in photo and outline candies with silver dragées.

- 9 cupcakes
- 11 mini cupcakes
- Pink frosting
- 3 Strawberry Ring Pops
- Silver dragées
- Pink and purple skittles

Friendly Whale

- *13 cupcakes*
- *5 mini cupcakes*
- *Blue frosting*
- *White frosting*
- *Dark gray frosting*

1. Place each color of frosting in a quart-size ziplock bag with the corner snipped off.

2. Pipe blue frosting in a spiral onto each cupcake, except for 3 of the mini cupcakes. Pipe white frosting on the 3 remaining mini cupcakes.

3. On a serving platter, arrange the blue cupcakes in a whale shape by making a row of 4 topped with an offset row of 4 topped with a row of 3. Place 2 cupcakes for the tail. Top the tail with two blue mini cupcakes.

4. Pipe a circle of white frosting on the whale for the eye. Make the spout by placing three white mini cupcakes in a "Y" shape over the middle cupcakes in the top row.

5. Using gray frosting, outline the whale. Outline the eye and add a gray pupil. Pipe a smile onto the whale.

Teddy

1. Place each color of frosting in a ziplock bag with the corner snipped off. Starting in the center of each cupcake, pipe chocolate frosting onto the cupcake in spirals. Frost all cupcakes with chocolate frosting.

2. On a serving platter, arrange the cupcakes in a bear shape, using 2 cupcakes at the top, followed by 3, then 2, then 3, then 3, then 2, then 2. Place 2 cupcakes at the sides for paws and 2 mini cupcakes at the top for ears.

3. Pipe tan frosting in spirals on the paws, feet, and ears. Pipe a large circle in the center for the tummy. Pipe on the face in an oval for the snout.

4. Pipe white frosting for the eyes and outline them in tan.

5. Use black gel frosting on the eyes to make pupils. Pipe a black nose and mouth.

- *19 cupcakes*
- *2 mini cupcakes*
- *Chocolate frosting*
- *Tan frosting*
- *White frosting*
- *1 tube black gel frosting*

Little Monsters

- *30 mini cupcakes*
- *Blue frosting*
- *Yellow fruit slices candy*
- *Green frosting*
- *White frosting*
- *1 tube black gel frosting*
- *Candy corn*

1. Arrange 15 mini cupcakes in a monster shape by placing 3 at the top, then 4 underneath, then 3, then 3, and then 2 for the feet. Place the blue frosting in a decorating bag with a star tip or hair/grass tip. Cover the entire monster with blue frosting.

2. Arrange the remaining 15 mini cupcakes in a second monster shape by placing 3 at the top, then 5, then 3, and then 2 for the feet. Place the 2 remaining cupcakes at the top. Place the green frosting in a decorating bag with a star tip or hair/grass tip. Cover the entire monster with green frosting. Place a yellow fruit slice on each of the 2 top cupcakes for horns.

3. Place the white frosting in a decorating bag with a round tip or a ziplock bag with the corner snipped off. Draw 2 eyes on the blue monster and 3 eyes on the green monster using white frosting. Draw pupils using black gel frosting, then add a white dot to each pupil. Draw smiles using white frosting.

Cut off the white ends from several pieces of candy corn. Place the white ends along each smile for teeth.

Cut off the yellow ends of 6 pieces of candy corn. Discard the yellow ends. Stick the orange and white ends into the blue monster's hands for claws.

Dump Truck

1 Arrange the cupcakes in a truck shape by placing a row of 6 along the bottom, then a row of 7, then a row of 6, then a row of 5. Place 2 cupcakes at the bottom for wheels.

2 Frost the main body of the truck with yellow frosting. Spread the frosting smooth with a knife. Place the orange frosting in a decorating bag with a round tip or a ziplock bag with the corner snipped off. Outline the dump bin shape and then fill in with orange frosting. Spread the frosting smooth with a knife.

3 Frost the wheels with black frosting. Place the remaining black frosting in a decorating bag with a round tip or a ziplock bag with the corner snipped off. Draw black wheel wells above the wheels. Draw a window and fill in with black frosting.

- 26 cupcakes
- Yellow frosting
- Orange frosting
- Black frosting
- White frosting
- Chocolate sandwich cookies

4 Place the white frosting in a decorating bag with a round tip or a ziplock bag with the corner snipped off. Outline the truck, dump bin, window, and wheel wells. Draw a circle in the center of each wheel. Fill in the circles with orange frosting.

5 Crush the sandwich cookies in a food processor. Sprinkle the crumbs in the dump bin.

Cuddly Koala

- *29 mini cupcakes*
- *5 cupcakes*
- *Gray frosting*
- *Chocolate frosting*
- *White frosting*
- *Brown peanut M&Ms*
- *1 tube black gel frosting*
- *Green frosting*

1. Frost 24 mini cupcakes gray. Arrange the frosted cupcakes in a koala shape according to the photo. Use 4 cupcakes at the top, followed by 3, then 2, then 3, then 5, then 3, then 4.

2. Place the white frosting in a decorating bag with a hair/grass tip or star tip. Frost the ears white. Make white circles for the eyes and smooth out the frosting. Place brown peanut M&Ms in the center for pupils. Outline the koala and draw a nose and claws using black gel frosting.

3. Place the unfrosted regular-size cupcakes along the right side of the koala to form a tree branch. Place the remaining mini cupcakes along the tree branch for leaves. Place the chocolate frosting in a decorating bag with a round tip or a ziplock bag with the corner snipped off. Pipe vertical lines of frosting along the tree branch until it is completely covered.

4. Place the green frosting in a decorating bag with a round tip or a ziplock bag with the corner snipped off. Draw leaves with frosting.

Soccer Ball

1 Frost 13 cupcakes with white frosting.

2 Place the black frosting in a decorating bag with a round tip or a ziplock bag with the corner snipped off. Place 5 evenly spaced dots of black frosting around the edges of 1 cupcake. Connect the dots with lines of black frosting. You should have a pentagon (5-sided) shape. Fill in the pentagon with black frosting. Frost the remaining 6 regular-size cupcakes in the same way with black frosting.

3 On a serving platter, arrange the cupcakes in a soccer ball shape by placing a black cupcake in the center, surrounded by 7 white cupcakes. Then place the remaining cupcakes along the outside edge, alternating between black and white.

4 Place the mini cupcakes in a rough pattern along the outside edge of the ball.

- *20 cupcakes*
- *12 mini cupcakes*
- *White frosting*
- *Black frosting*
- *Green frosting*

5 Place the green frosting in a decorating bag with a round tip. Pipe a circle around the soccer ball a few inches in from the outside edge. Replace the round decorating tip with a star tip or grass/hair tip. Cover the area from the green line to the outside edges of the cupcakes in green grass.

Flower Bouquet ● ● ● ● ● ●

1 Place each color of frosting in a decorating
bag with a round tip or a ziplock bag with the
corner snipped off. Starting in the center of each
cupcake, pipe frosting onto the cupcake in round
spirals. Frost 5 cupcakes purple, 10 pink, and 5
yellow. Pipe the green frosting in oval spirals on
the remaining 4 cupcakes.

2 On a serving platter, arrange the cupcakes
into 3 flowers, using 5 cupcakes for the
petals and 1 yellow cupcake for each center.
Place a piece of green licorice at the bottom
of each flower for the stem. Place the green
cupcakes against the stems for leaves.

3 To make the bumblebees, pipe a line of
black gel frosting across the bottom of each
of the 2 remaining yellow cupcakes. Pipe 2 lines
of black gel frosting across the centers. Pipe a
circle at the top for the heads. Place 2 white
conversation hearts on each side for the wings.
Cut small strips of black licorice for the stingers

- 24 mini cupcakes
- Purple frosting
- Pink frosting
- Yellow frosting
- Green frosting
- Green licorice
- 1 tube black gel frosting
- White conversation hearts
- Black licorice
- Mini chocolate chips (optional)

and antennae. Stick a stinger into the frosting at the bottom of each cupcake. Stick two antennae into the frosting head. Place the bumblebees above the flowers.

4 If desired, create "flight paths" by carefully placing mini chocolate chips into curvy lines from the flowers to the bumblebees.

Fun Flip-Flops

- *22 mini cupcakes*
- *Yellow frosting*
- *Hot pink frosting*
- *Light green frosting*
- *Hot pink licorice*

1. Arrange 11 mini cupcakes into a flip-flop shape, placing 4 vertically along the right side, then 5, then 2. Repeat with the remaining 11 cupcakes, reversing the order so that the 4 cupcakes are along the left edge and the 2 cupcakes are along the right edge.

2. Place the yellow frosting in a decorating bag with a round tip or a ziplock bag with the corner snipped off. Draw an outline around each flip-flop. Fill in the outlines with yellow frosting, completely covering the cupcakes and gaps.

3. Place the hot pink frosting in a decorating bag with a drop flower tip. Pipe flowers on the flip-flops. Place the light green frosting in a decorating bag with a leaf tip and pipe leaves onto the flowers.

4. Cut the licorice into 4 pieces about 4 inches long each. Stick two pieces into each flip-flop for the straps.

Happy Hippo

1. Frost 13 cupcakes and the 2 mini cupcakes with purple frosting. Frost the 3 remaining cupcakes with light purple frosting.

2. On a serving platter, arrange the cupcakes in a hippo shape, placing 2 purple cupcakes at the top, then 3 light purple cupcakes underneath, then 4 purple, then 3 purple, then 4 purple. Place the 2 mini cupcakes at the top for ears.

3. Place the remaining light purple frosting in a decorating bag with a round tip or a ziplock bag with the corner snipped off. Draw nostrils on the hippo and fill in with frosting. Use light purple frosting to make the jaw bigger along the bottom. Fill in any gaps in the jaw with light purple frosting and smooth with a knife.

4. Stick the two pieces of gum into the bottom of the jaw.

5. Place the white frosting in a decorating bag with a round tip or a ziplock bag with the

- *16 cupcakes*
- *2 mini cupcakes*
- *Purple frosting*
- *Light purple frosting*
- *White square gum*
- *White frosting*
- *Purple Spree candies*
- *Black licorice drops*

corner snipped off. Draw eyes above the jaw. Place a purple Spree candy onto each eye for the pupil, then add a dot of white frosting to each pupil. Pipe on light purple eyebrows over the eyes.

6 Place a purple Spree candy on each nostril. Place black licorice drops onto the arms and legs for toes.

Pretty Butterfly

1. Frost 6 cupcakes with black frosting. Frost the remaining cupcakes with green frosting.

2. Arrange the cupcakes in a butterfly shape: Place the 6 black cupcakes in the center. Place a vertical row of 5 green cupcakes on the right side. Add 2 more rows of 5 green cupcakes, placing each one higher than the last. Place a vertical row of 2 cupcakes along the right side at the top, placing them a little lower than the top of the last row.

3. Repeat the arrangement of the green cupcakes on the opposite side of the butterfly.

4. Fill in any gaps on the wings with more green frosting. Smooth the frosting with a knife.

5. Place the blue frosting in a decorating bag with a round tip or a ziplock bag with the

- *40 mini cupcakes*
- *Black frosting*
- *Green frosting*
- *Blue frosting*
- *Pink frosting*
- *Black licorice ropes*
- *Pink Wild Berry Skittles*

corner snipped off. Outline the wings with blue frosting, then draw blue swirls on the wings. Place the pink frosting in a decorating bag with a round tip or a ziplock bag with the corner snipped off. Pipe pink swirls next to the blue swirls.

6   Place pink Skittles on the wings.

7   Cut the black licorice ropes into 2 pieces about 4 to 5 inches each. Curl the ends by twisting the licorice around your finger. Place the licorice at the top of the head for antennae.

Nest of Bluebirds

1. Frost 6 cupcakes with light blue frosting. Frost the remaining cupcakes with chocolate frosting.

2. Arrange the chocolate frosted cupcakes in a nest shape by placing 4 in a row for the bottom, 5 in a row for the middle, and 6 in a row for the top.

3. Place the remaining chocolate frosting in a decorating bag with a round tip or a ziplock bag with the corner snipped off. Pipe lines of frosting in random directions for twigs. Place the green frosting in a decorating bag with a round tip and draw leaves on the nest.

4. Cut 3 orange Skittles in half and place 2 pieces on a blue frosted cupcake for a beak. Repeat with the remaining Skittles pieces and 2 more blue cupcakes. Cut the gumdrop in half and place 1 half on a blue cupcake for the mama bird's beak.

5. Place the birds at the top of the nest. Draw eyes and wings using black gel frosting.

- *21 cupcakes*
- *Light blue frosting*
- *Chocolate frosting*
- *Green frosting*
- *Orange Skittles*
- *Orange gumdrop*
- *1 tube black gel frosting*

Wizard's Hat · · · · · · · ·

- *22 cupcakes*
- *Dark purple frosting*
- *Yellow frosting*
- *Yellow decorating sugar*

1 Frost the cupcakes with dark purple frosting. Arrange the cupcakes in a hat shape by placing 6 cupcakes in a row at the bottom, then 5, then 4, then 3, then 2, then 1, then 1. Add more purple frosting to fill in any gaps and smooth the frosting with a knife.

2 Place the yellow frosting in a decorating bag with a round tip or a ziplock bag with the corner snipped off. Draw stars and moons on the hat. Draw trim along the bottom of the hat. Sprinkle the hat with yellow decorating sugar.

Polka-Dot Dinosaur

1 Frost the cupcakes with green frosting. Arrange the cupcakes in a dinosaur shape. Fill in any gaps with more green frosting and smooth with a knife.

2 Place the yellow frosting in a decorating bag with a round tip or a ziplock bag with the corner snipped off. Outline the dinosaur with yellow frosting. Outline toes with yellow frosting. Place the blue frosting in a decorating bag with a round tip. Fill in toes with blue frosting. Decorate dinosaur with yellow and blue gumballs.

3 Place the white frosting in a decorating bag with a round tip and draw the dinosaur's eye.

4 Cut the bottoms off 2 black licorice drops. Place 1 piece on the head for the nostril and 1 piece on the eye for the pupil. Add a dot of white frosting to the pupil.

5 Cut each Starburst candy in half diagonally to make triangles. Place the triangles along the dinosaur's neck, back, and tail.

- *26 cupcakes*
- *Green frosting*
- *Yellow frosting*
- *Blue frosting*
- *Blue and yellow gumballs*
- *White frosting*
- *Black licorice drops*
- *Yellow Starburst candies*

Spotted Puppy

- 20 cupcakes
- White frosting
- Chocolate frosting
- Black licorice drops
- Red Twizzlers Pull-n-Peel licorice
- 1 yellow Giant Sweet Tarts candy

Frost 16 cupcakes with white frosting. Frost the remaining 4 cupcakes with chocolate frosting.

Place 1 white cupcake surrounded by 6 white cupcakes for the puppy's head. Place 2 chocolate cupcakes on each side for ears. Make the puppy's body by placing a row of 2 white cupcakes, then 3, then 4.

Place the remaining chocolate frosting in a decorating bag with a round tip. Draw spots on the dog and fill in with frosting. Draw lines on the feet to create toes. Draw one large spot on the face where one of the eyes will be.

Place 2 black licorice drops on the face for the eyes, putting one drop in the center of the brown spot. Place a licorice drop under the eyes for the nose.

Cut a piece of licorice about 5 inches long. Place around the neck. Place the yellow Sweet Tart under the licorice for the tag. Write the name on the tag in frosting if desired.

Sparkly Snowflakes

1. Frost the cupcakes with light blue frosting. On a serving platter, arrange the cupcakes into a snowflake: Place 1 cupcake in the center and surround with 6 cupcakes. Place 2 cupcakes vertically above each of the 6 cupcakes. Repeat to make a second smaller snowflake, this time placing just 1 cupcake above each of the 6 center cupcakes.

2. Place the white frosting in a decorating bag with a round tip or a ziplock bag with the corner snipped off. Draw geometric designs on the snowflakes. Sprinkle the snowflakes with sugar crystals.

- *32 mini cupcakes*
- *Light blue frosting*
- *White frosting*
- *Coarse sugar crystals*

Pokey the Hedgehog

- *15 mini cupcakes*
- *Chocolate frosting*
- *Large chocolate chips*
- *White frosting*
- *Black licorice drops*

1 Frost the cupcakes with chocolate frosting. On a serving platter, arrange the cupcakes in a hedgehog shape by placing a row of 4 at the top, then a row of 5 for the middle, then a row of 6 for the bottom. Fill in any gaps with more chocolate frosting and smooth with a knife.

2 Place chocolate chips over most of the top, leaving the part uncovered where the hedgehog's face will be.

3 Place the white frosting in a decorating bag with a round tip or a ziplock bag with the corner snipped off. Pipe a circle on the hedgehog's face for the eye. Place an upside-down chocolate chip on the eye for the pupil. Pipe a small dot of white frosting on the pupil.

4 Place an upside-down chocolate chip on the face for the nose.

5 Place black licorice drops on the bottom of the hedgehog for the feet.

Pretty Pony

- *33 mini cupcakes*
- *White frosting*
- *Pink frosting*
- *Black frosting*

1 On a serving platter, arrange the cupcakes in a pony shape according to the photo: Place a horizontal row of 3, followed by a row of 3 for the pony's body. Place two rows of 3 vertically in a slightly curved shape for the pony's back legs. Place a row of 5 vertically to the right of the row of 2, then place a row of 6 vertically next to that, only a little higher, to make the pony's front legs. Place two vertical rows of 3 to make the pony's face. Place 1 cupcake to make the nose. Place 3 cupcakes in a curved line to the left of the pony's body to make the tail.

2 Place the white frosting in a decorating bag with a round tip or a ziplock bag with the corner snipped off. Pipe frosting in spirals onto all the cupcakes except the mane and tail.

3 Place the pink frosting in a decorating bag with a round tip or a ziplock bag with the corner snipped off. Pipe lines on the unfrosted cupcakes to create the mane and tail.

4 Spread pink frosting on the bottom of each leg for the hooves.

5 Place the black frosting in a decorating bag with a round tip or a ziplock bag with the corner snipped off. Draw a nostril and an eye on the horse's face. Draw the bridle and bit using thick lines of black frosting.

Treasure Chest

- 21 cupcakes

- Chocolate frosting

- 11 mini cupcakes

- Yellow frosting

- Yellow M&Ms

- White gumballs

- Hard candies

- Rolos

1 Frost the regular-size cupcakes with chocolate frosting. Frost the mini cupcakes with yellow frosting.

2 On a serving platter, arrange the chocolate-frosted cupcakes in a treasure chest shape: Place 3 rows of 4 cupcakes each for the front of the chest. For the right side of the chest, place a vertical row of 5 cupcakes to the right of the rows and up a little. For the lid of the chest, place a horizontal row of 4 cupcakes to the left of the top cupcake. Fill the inside of the chest with yellow mini cupcakes.

3 Place the remaining yellow frosting in a decorating bag with a basketweave tip. Using the smooth side of the tip, outline the edges of the chest. Draw a yellow square at the top center of the front of the chest. Place yellow M&Ms along the yellow lines.

4 Make a pearl necklace using white gumballs. Place hard candies and Rolos on top of the yellow cupcakes.

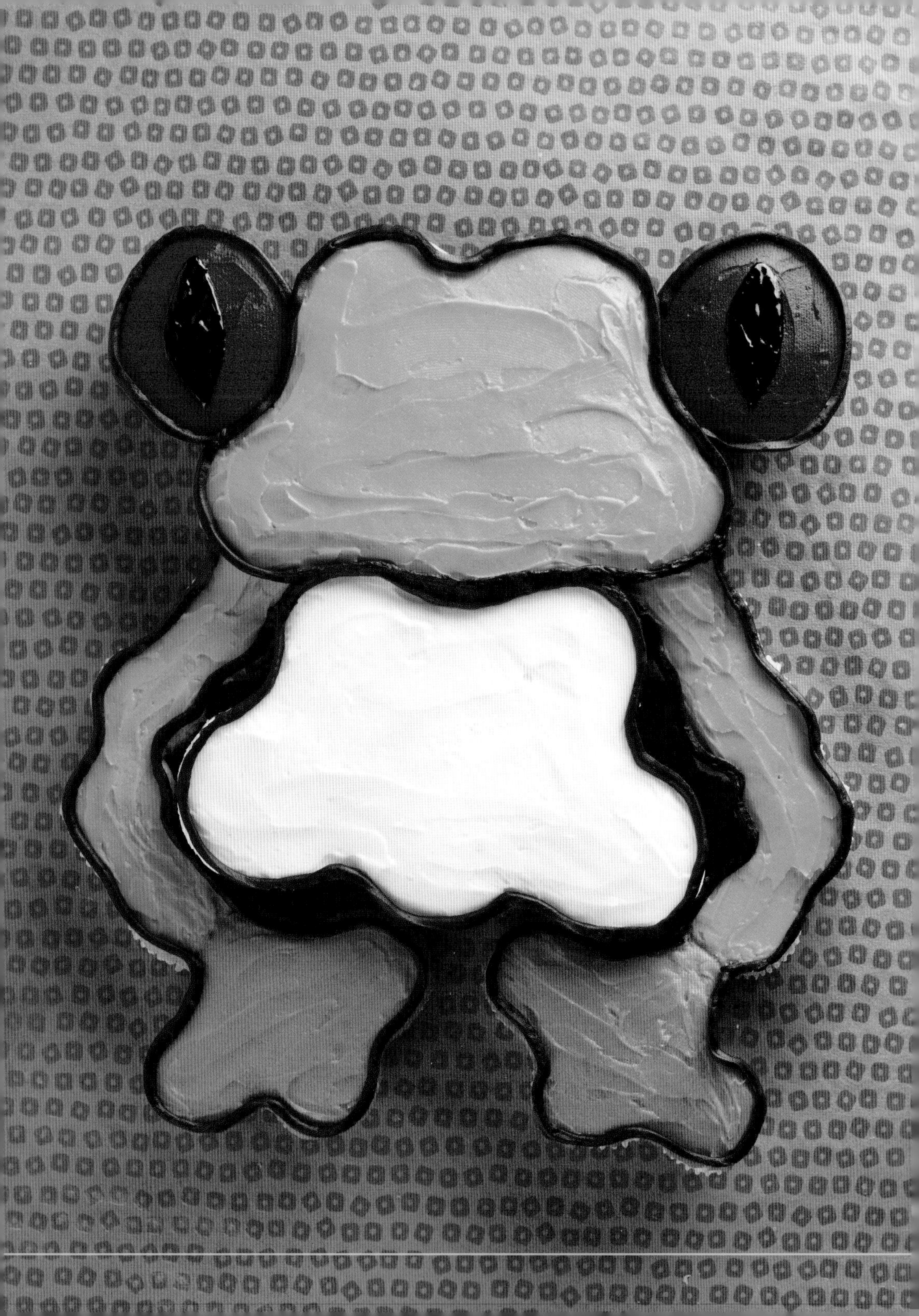

Tree Frog

1 Frost 5 cupcakes and 8 mini cupcakes with green frosting. Frost 5 cupcakes with white frosting. Frost 2 cupcakes with red frosting. Frost 8 mini cupcakes with orange frosting.

2 Arrange the cupcakes in a frog shape: Place 2 green cupcakes at the top followed by 3 green, then 2 white, then 3 white. Place a red cupcake on either side of the face for the eyes. Place 4 mini green cupcakes on either side of the body for the arms. Place an orange mini cupcake at the end of each arm and surround it with 3 orange mini cupcakes for the hands.

3 Place the dark gray frosting in a decorating bag with a round tip or a ziplock bag with the corner snipped off. Draw pupils on the red eyes. Draw an outline around the frog. Draw a line between the green and white cupcakes for the mouth.

- *12 cupcakes*
- *16 mini cupcakes*
- *Green frosting*
- *White frosting*
- *Orange frosting*
- *Red frosting*
- *Dark gray frosting*

Owl

- 19 cupcakes
- Chocolate frosting
- White frosting
- Keebler 100 Calorie Right Bites Pecan Sandies
- 2 scallop-edged shortbread cookies
- 3 orange slices candies

1. On a serving platter, arrange the cupcakes in an owl shape by placing a row of 4 at the top, then a row of 3, then a row of 3, then a row of 4, then a row of 3, then a row of 2.

2. Frost the owl with white frosting, except for the outside edges.

3. Place the chocolate frosting in a decorating bag with a round tip or a ziplock bag with the corner snipped off. Outline the face and sides of the owl and fill in with more lines.

4. Place Pecan Sandies on the stomach of the owl for feathers.

5. Place 2 shortbread cookies for the eyes. Pipe a circle of chocolate frosting in the center of each eye.

6. Place an orange slice on the face for the beak. Place two orange slices at the bottom of the owl for the feet.

Seahorse

- 27 mini cupcakes
- Orange frosting
- Orange slices candies
- White frosting
- Tube of black gel frosting
- Green frosting

1. On a serving platter, arrange 20 of the cupcakes in a seahorse shape: Place 2 at the top, followed by 2 below and slightly to the right, then 2 more below and slightly to the right, then 3, then 3, then 2. Add 4 cupcakes in a curved line at the bottom for the tail. Add 2 cupcakes to the left of the head for the nose.

2. Place the orange frosting in a decorating bag with a round tip or a ziplock bag with the corner snipped off. Pipe spirals onto each cupcake of the seahorse.

3. Carefully cut out the center of each orange slice to make a deeper crescent shape. Place the orange slices along the back and tail of the seahorse to create a ridged back.

4. Place the white frosting in a decorating bag with a round tip or a ziplock bag with the corner snipped off. Pipe a circle for the eye. Draw a pupil on the eye using black frosting. Place a dot of white frosting on the pupil.

Place the green frosting in a decorating bag
with a round tip or a ziplock bag with the
corner snipped off. Pipe a leaf shape onto each of
the unfrosted cupcakes. Arrange the cupcakes in
a seaweed shape next to the seahorse.

Lollipops

- 21 mini cupcakes
- White frosting
- Red frosting
- Orange frosting
- Yellow frosting
- Green frosting
- Blue frosting
- White straws

1. Arrange cupcakes in a lollipop shape by placing 1 cupcake in the center, surrounded by 6 cupcakes. Repeat two more times to make 2 more lollipops.

2. Place each color of frosting in a ziplock bag with the corner snipped off.

3. To make the center lollipop, use white frosting to draw a curved line from the center of the lollipop to the outside edge. Repeat 4 more times to make a total of 5 curved lines. Use each color of frosting to fill in the spaces between the lines.

4. To make the left lollipop, use red frosting to pipe a very loose spiral, starting at the center. Repeat with yellow, green, and blue frosting, placing each spiral next to the previous one. Add more curved lines of frosting on the outsides of the lollipop to fill in any unfrosted areas. Pipe a few spirals of white frosting on top.

Repeat step 4 to make the remaining
lollipop, this time using orange, yellow, green,
blue, and white frosting.

Place a straw underneath each lollipop for
the stick.

Collect Them All!